Arctic Ocean

30°E    60°    90°    120°    150°

A

EUROPE

S    I    A

IRAN

A

Pacific

Ocean

AFRICA

Indian

Ocean

AUSTRALIA

ANTARCTICA

# *Iran*

## Leon Gray

Edmund Herzig and Dorreh Mirheydar, Consultants

**NATIONAL GEOGRAPHIC**

WASHINGTON, D.C.

# Contents

# Foreword

Iran has a wide variety of physical landscapes, although that might not be immediately clear from looking at a map of the country. Heading north along the scenic Chalus Road, travelers pass through a landscape similar to that of Switzerland. Beside the northern slopes of the Elburz Range is the rice, tea, olive, and cotton-growing lowland of the Caspian Sea, which has Mediterranean scenery. In the west, through the beautiful valleys of the Zagros Mountains, lie stunning landscapes that Iranians call "the Hidden Paradise." In the east, tourists are attracted by the unique characteristics and scattered settlements of Dasht-i-Kavir and Dasht-i-Lut. Traveling southwest into the fertile plain of Khuzistan, with its hot and humid climate and burning fields of oil and gas, one is reminded of Texas.

Iran has long been known to the West as the land of poetry, songs, the rose, and the nightingale. Iranians are traditionally lovers of poetry, music, and rose gardens. The long poem *Shahnameh* ("The Epic of Kings"), written by Ferdowsi over a thousand years ago, is very popular among ordinary Iranians. So too are the poems of Saadi, Hafez, and Molavi, which are more philosophical and romantic.

Words by Saadi are quoted on the entrance to the Hall of Nations at the United Nations headquarters in New York. They express the idea that all humankind is joined, and that an injury to one part of the human race is an injury to all:

> "Of one Essence is the human race,
> Thusly has Creation put the Base;
> One Limb impacted is sufficient,
> For all Others to feel the Mace."

In the early 20th century, Iran joined the modern world by transforming its political and administrative structure. The hardships of two world wars ruined the economy, however. After the middle of the 20th century it took Iran 30 years to become a major player in political and economic affairs of the region. Under the Islamic Republic created in 1979, people have become more politically minded, due in large part to the government policy that politics and religion cannot be separated. Now, even ordinary Iranians take notice of state affairs and are urged to express their views on various matters.

Iran has traditionally played a powerful role in politics of southwest Asia. There are no reasons that this will not continue in the future.

▲ The new building of the National Library in Tehran is one of the largest libraries in the Middle East.

*Dorreh Mirheydar*

Dorreh Mirheydar
*University of Tehran*

# Varied
## and
# Beautiful
# Land

IRAN IS CUT OFF FROM THE OUTSIDE world by its beautiful but often desolate landscape. The east of the country is covered by a lifeless and salty desert. The western region is surrounded by mountain ranges that create a rugged barrier between Iran and its neighbors. The northern and southern frontiers are formed by shorelines.

Iran's hugely varied landscape shapes the lives of its people. Lush coastal regions form the main farming centers. Most Iranians live in sprawling cities scattered across a central plateau. The plateau runs across the middle of Iran between the mountains, seas, and desert. The cityscape of Tehran, Iran's capital, mirrors that of any Western nation, but much of Iran is a truly wild environment untouched by human development.

◀ Apartment buildings rise above a suburb of Tehran, with the snow-capped peaks of the Elburz Mountains looming even higher above the city.

At a Glance

# WHAT'S THE WEATHER LIKE?

Iran has contrasting climates thanks to its varied landscape. In the western mountains, the summer is dry and hot but the winter is freezing cold. The central plateau is dry with a hot summer and cooler winter. Most water there comes from melting winter snows in the mountains. By contrast, the northern coast has a warm and wet climate.

The map opposite shows the physical features of Iran. Labels on this map and on similar maps throughout this book identify most of the places pictured in each chapter.

## Fast Facts

**OFFICIAL NAME:** Islamic Republic of Iran

**FORM OF GOVERNMENT:** Islamic Republic

**CAPITAL:** Tehran

**POPULATION:** 70,472,846

**OFFICIAL LANGUAGE:** Farsi

**MONETARY UNIT:** rial

**TOTAL AREA:** 636,372 square miles (1,648,105 square kilometers)

**BORDERING NATIONS:** Afghanistan, Armenia, Azerbaijan, Iraq, Pakistan, Turkey, Turkmenistan

**HIGHEST POINT:** Mount Damavand, 18,606 feet (5,671 meters)

**LOWEST POINT:** Caspian Sea, –92 feet (–28 meters)

**MAJOR RIVERS:** Karun, Karkeh, Zayandeh

**LARGEST LAKE:** Lake Urmia, 2,000 square miles (5,200 square kilometers)

## Average Temperature & Rainfall

Average High/Low Temperatures; Yearly Rainfall

**TEHRAN (NORTH):**
73°F (23°C) / 57°F (14°C); 13 in (33 cm)

**ESFAHAN (CENTRAL):**
75°F (24°C) / 46°F (8°C); 4 in (11 cm)

**TABRIZ (NORTHWEST):**
65°F (18°C) / 45°F (7°C); 12 in (31 cm)

**BANDAR-E 'ABBAS (SOUTH):**
90°F (32°C) / 72°F (22°C); 3 in (8 cm)

Caspian Sea

Zagros Mountains

Persian Gulf

Gulf of Oman

0 mi 200
0 km 200

MAP KEY
Dry — Arid
Semiarid
Coastal
Mild — Mediterranean
Highland — Highland

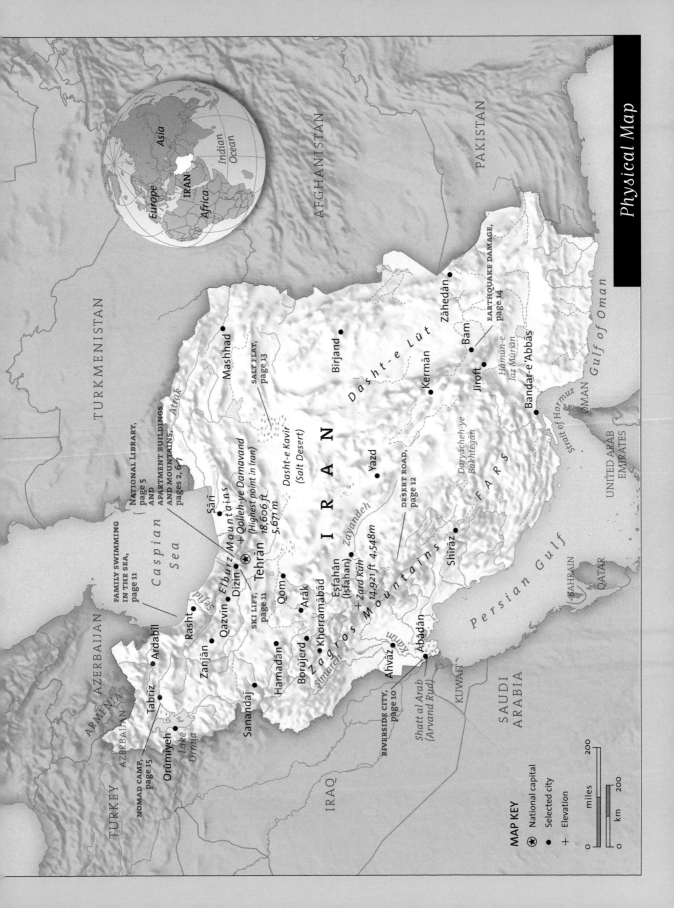

Physical Map

TURKEY

ARMENIA

AZERBAIJAN

TURKMENISTAN

AFGHANISTAN

PAKISTAN

Europe

Asia

IRAN

Africa

Indian
Ocean

NOMAD CAMP,
page 15

Orūmīyeh

Lake
Urmia

AZERBAIJAN

Tabriz

Ardabīl

FAMILY SWIMMING
IN THE SEA, page 11

Caspian
Sea

Rasht

Safīd

Sefīd

Sārī

NATIONAL LIBRARY,
page 5
AND
APARTMENT BUILDINGS
AND MOUNTAINS,
pages 2, 6, 7

Elburz Mountains

+ Qolleh-ye Damāvand
(Highest point in Iran)
18,606 ft
5,671 m

Atrak

Mashhad

Sanandaj

Zanjān

Qazvīn

Dizin

Tehrān ⊛

SKI LIFT,
page 11

Hamadān

Qom

Borūjerd

Arāk

Khorramābād

Esfahān
(Isfahan)

Zāyandeh

+ Zard Kūh
14,921 ft 4,548m

SALT FLAT,
page 13

Dasht-e Kavīr
(Salt Desert)

Yazd

Birjand

Dasht-e Lūt

Zāhedān

EARTHQUAKE DAMAGE,
page 14

Kermān

Bam

Zagros Mountains

Sīmareh

Shiraz

FARS

Daryācheh-ye
Bakhtegān

Jīroft

Hāmūn-e
Jaz Mūriān

Bandar-e 'Abbās

Karun

Ahvāz

Ābādān

DESERT ROAD,
page 12

IRAQ

KUWAIT

Shatt al Arab
(Arvand Rud)

RIVERSIDE CITY,
page 10

Persian Gulf

BAHRAIN

QATAR

SAUDI
ARABIA

UNITED ARAB
EMIRATES

OMAN

Strait of Hormuz

Gulf of Oman

I R A N

MAP KEY

⊛ National capital

• Selected city

+ Elevation

miles                200

0

km                 200

0

▲ The city of Abadan sits on the Iranian side of the Shatt al Arab. The other bank belongs to Iraq. The waterway is one of the largest in the Middle East and is an important shipping route.

# At the Heart of the Region

Iran's location in southwest Asia gives it a central role in a vast area that extends north to include the regions of Central Asia and Caucasia, east to Afghanistan and Pakistan, and west to the Arab states of the Middle East. The whole area is often known as the Greater Middle East. For millennia, Iran—formerly known as Persia—has been a meeting place for peoples and cultures from throughout the region.

Iran's western border has traditionally marked the boundary between the Arab and non-Arab countries of West Asia. In the past, it shifted frequently as the two cultures clashed. Today, the conflict is echoed in a dispute over a large waterway the Iranians call Arvand Rud but which is better known as the Shatt al Arab. Iran shares the Shatt al Arab with its neighbor, Iraq, but the two countries argue about the exact position of their borders. The Shatt al Arab gives access to the

Persian Gulf. The Persian Gulf, and the Gulf of Oman beyond, are Iran's shipping gateway to the Indian Ocean.

## Peaks above Plateaus

Much of Iran's land is far above sea level. Mountains surround high and flat areas known as the central plateau. The Zagros Mountains tower over the western half of the country, sweeping from Azerbaijan province in the northwest to the Persian Gulf in the southeast. Many peaks in the range top 9,600 feet (3,000 m). The highest peak, Zard Kuh, reaches 14,921 feet (4,548 m). High cliffs and steep canyons make the range impassable after heavy snow falls during the winter.

▲ Skiers ride in a cable car at Dizin, a popular resort in the Elburz Mountains near Tehran. In the background rises Mount Damavand, Iran's highest peak.

## LANDLOCKED SEA

The Caspian Sea is the world's largest lake. It forms part of Iran's northern border and is also surrounded by Kazakhstan, Turkmenistan, Russia, and Azerbaijan. The sea is fed from the north by the mighty Volga and Ural Rivers. Iran's short Sefid River also flows from the Elburz Mountains into the sea. The water entering the sea is fresh but much of it evaporates, leaving salt behind. As a result the Caspian's water tastes a little salty. The amount of water that reaches the sea fluctuates greatly from year to year. That changes the shape of Iran's northern coastline as the water level rises and falls.

▲ An Iranian family bathes in the Caspian Sea. Religious rules do not allow women to wear bathing suits when men are present.

▲ A single road crosses the dry interior of Iran, which shimmers with heat on the northern edge of the Zagros Mountains.

The Elburz Mountains are a narrower but even higher range near the northern border. They form a barrier between the Central Plateau and the Caspian Sea. The Elburz contains Iran's highest peak, the towering Qolleh-ye Damavand (Mount Damavand).

## WILD WINDS

Every summer, from the end of May to late September, Sistan and Baluchestan province, a dry region in the southeastern corner of Iran, experiences strong northerly winds known as the "wind of 120 days." The wind blows day and night, sometimes nearly reaching hurricane force—up to 70 miles (120 km) per hour. The winds originate from bad weather in India. Huge sandstorms created by the winds are very destructive, eating away buildings and turning water supplies into mud.

## *Empty Lands*

Two of the world's driest deserts cover the eastern Central Plateau. The Dasht-e Lut, or "Barren Desert," is one of the hottest places on Earth. During the brief wet season, water flows into the desert from the Zagros Mountains, but creeks soon dry up in the heat to leave salt flats, sand, and rocks.

Between the Dasht-e Lut and the Elburz Mountains in the north stretches the Dasht-e Kavir, or "Great Salt Desert." The Dasht-e Kavir is dry for most of the year, but

# A LANDSCAPE OF SALT

The salt flats of the Dasht-e Kavir are not the only feature of the Iranian landscape formed by salt. In the mountains rise salt domes. They are created when layers of salt buried for millions of years gradually push back up through the rock. The domes formed by the salt can be more than 1,000 feet (330 meters) high.

▶ A salt flat, or *kavir*, in eastern Iran. The flats are not solid, which makes crossing them difficult.

small streams create lakes and salt swamps in the winter and spring. One road crosses the heart of the two deserts, but otherwise the area is impassable.

## Low and Lush

Iran has two lowland areas—the Caspian coast and the Khuzestan plain in the southwest. The Caspian coast is a long, narrow strip of land between the sea and the slopes of the Elburz Mountains. The region enjoys a subtropical climate. It rarely gets very cold and receives plenty of rain, making the soils very fertile. Farmers have cleared much of the natural forest to grow crops such as cotton, tea, and rice.

Khuzestan is a lowland strip between the Shatt al Arab and the foothills of the Zagros Mountains that runs into Iraq. The Khuzestan plain contains most of Iran's deposits of petroleum and natural gas.

▼ Iranian tea is traditionally served without milk in glass beakers. Tea-growing began in the hills near the Caspian coast in the late 1800s, where the climate was perfect for the tea plants.

## Precious Water

In a hot country with no large rivers, water is precious. Apart from the Shatt al Arab (Arvand Rud), the only Iranian river wide enough for cargo and passenger boats is the Karun. The Karun is fed by melted snow from the central Zagros Mountains and flows south across Khuzestan to the Shatt al Arab. Other smaller

## EARTHQUAKE ZONE

The mountain ranges that sweep across Iran are growing taller as sections, or plates, of Earth's surface ram into each other deep underground. These collisions provide the enormous forces behind the many earthquakes and volcanoes in the country. One of the most devastating earthquakes in recent history occurred on December 26, 2003, which destroyed the ancient city of Bam in the east of Iran. More than 26,000 people were killed as their houses made of dried mud collapsed.

▶ The Citadel of Bam was built using mud and straw (*top*). In 2003, the 2,000-year-old Citadel was destroyed by an earthquake (*bottom*).

rivers drain into the Persian Gulf, while those that rise in the northern Zagros or Elburz drain into the Caspian Sea. On the Central Plateau, rivers run in spring, when the winter snows melt, but are dry for the rest of the year. Many of the plateau's rivers do not reach the sea. They flow into lakes, which grow in spring but shrink during the summer as the heat evaporates the water. As the water evaporates, minerals in the lake become more concentrated. The water becomes too salty for drinking or watering crops.

▲ A family of nomads sit with their belongings as they wait for others to take down their tents and prepare to move to a new site. About 5,000 Shahsavan nomads live near the border with Azerbaijan in northwestern Iran.

## A Mixture of Peoples

Iran is home to around 70 million people. As a major power in the Middle East, Iran is often mistaken for an Arab country. However, most Iranians are Farsi, part of an ethnic group who also live in Central Asia and western Afghanistan. Iran is home to people with other ethnic backgrounds, too. For example, 24 percent of Iranians are Azerbaijanis. They live in the northwest. Another large group are the Kurds, who live close to the border with Turkey and northern Iraq. Some Arabs also live in Iran, mainly in Khuzestan.

# The Living Landscape

**N**OT SO LONG AGO, IRAN WAS home to many lions, tigers, and other big cats. Unfortunately these sleek hunters are now very rare, and some have gone forever. Iran's last Asiatic lion was seen in 1941. (There are only 350 wild Asiatic lions left and they all live in India.) The Caspian tiger used to hunt in the forests of northern Iran. Although people report seeing tigers in the area on occasion, biologists think that the Caspian tiger is now extinct.

The two surviving Iranian big cats are the Asiatic cheetah and Persian leopard. Both are in danger of being wiped out as well. Around 60 cheetahs live in a national park north of the Kavir Desert. Persian leopards are found among the Elburz and Zagros Mountains. Nevertheless, there are just a few hundred individuals.

◀ **A Persian leopard feasts on an ibex mountain goat. Although they are rare, wild cheetahs sometimes attack sheep and goats and some get shot by herders.**

# NATIONAL PARKS

Iran has several national parks and many more protected areas. Golestan National Park is one of the oldest and largest of the reserves. This park in northeastern Iran is a mixture of thick forests, mountain passes, and dry plains. It is home to wild sheep and gazelles. The park is also a stronghold for Persian leopards. Kavir National Park lies on the western edge of the Dasht-e Kavir. The park covers a region called "Little Africa," because its plains support shrubs and wildlife similar to those of the African grassland. The park is the last home of the Asiatic cheetah.

Lake Urmia National Park in western Iran contains the largest lake in the Middle East. Wetlands which regularly dry out and flood again surround the lake. There are no fish in the lake because the water is too salty for them to survive. However, birds, such as flamingos and pelicans, come to the lake to feed on brine shrimp.

▲ The critically endangered Asiatic cheetah hunts antelope and gazelle by accelerating from 0 to 70 mph (0–110 kmh) in 3.5 seconds, quicker than most sports cars.

# Species at Risk

The following Iranian animals are listed as endangered by the World Conservation Union (IUCN):

- Asiatic black bear
- Asiatic cheetah
- Baluchistan bear
- Beluga sturgeon (fish)
- Euphrates softshell turtle
- Gorgan salamander
- Hawksbill turtle
- Iranian jerboa (mouse)
- Meadow's viper (snake)
- Persian fallow deer
- Persian mole
- Persian onager (ass)
- Slender-billed curlew (bird)
- Sociable lapwing (bird)
- White-rumped vulture

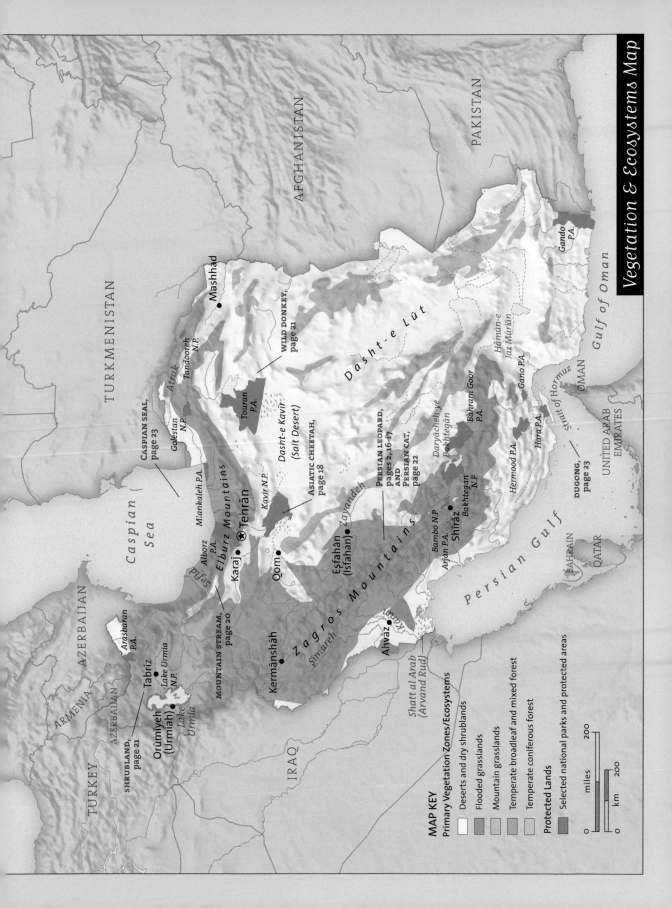

# Vegetation & Ecosystems Map

TURKEY

ARMENIA

AZERBAIJAN

**SHRUBLAND,**
**page 21**

*Arasbaran*
*P.A.*

Tabrīz

*Lake Urmia*
*N.P.*

Orūmīyeh
(Urmiah)

*Lake*
*Urmia*

AZERBAIJAN

IRAQ

Kermānshāh

*Zagros Mountains*

*Sīmareh*

Ahvāz

*Kārūn*

*Shatt al Arab*
*(Arvand Rud)*

**MOUNTAIN STREAM,**
**page 20**

*Sefīd*

Karaj

Qom

Esfahān
(Isfahan)

*Zayandeh*

**★** Tehrān

*Alborz*
*P.A.*

*Elburz Mountains*

*Miankaleh P.A.*

**CASPIAN SEAL,**
**page 23**

TURKMENISTAN

*Caspian*
*Sea*

*Atrak*

*Golestan*
*N.P.*

*Tandooreh*
*N.P.*

Mashhad

**WILD DONKEY,**
**page 21**

*Touran*
*P.A.*

*Dasht-e Kavir*
*(Salt Desert)*

*Kavir N.P.*

**ASIATIC CHEETAH,**
**page 18**

**PERSIAN LEOPARD,**
**pages 2,16-17**
**AND**
**PERSIAN CAT,**
**page 22**

AFGHANISTAN

*Dasht-e Lūt*

*Hāmūn-e*
*Jaz Mūriān*

PAKISTAN

*Gando*
*P.A.*

*Gulf of Oman*

*Strait of Hormuz*

OMAN

UNITED ARAB
EMIRATES

**DUGONG,**
**page 23**

*Hara P.A.*

*Gano P.A.*

*Bahram Goor*
*P.A.*

*Hermood P.A.*

*Daryācheh-ye*
*Bakhtegān*

*Bakhtegan*
*N.P*

Shīrāz

*Bambo N.P*

*Arjan P.A.*

*Persian Gulf*

BAHRAIN

QATAR

## MAP KEY

### Primary Vegetation Zones/Ecosystems

Deserts and dry shrublands

Flooded grasslands

Mountain grasslands

Temperate broadleaf and mixed forest

Temperate coniferous forest

Protected Lands

Selected national parks and protected areas

miles    200

0

km    200

0

## Wooded Mountains

Iran is dominated by high plains and steep mountain ranges. The flat areas of the Central Plateau are dry and empty, while the mountain slopes receive enough water for forests to grow. Most of Iran's wildlife lives on the tree-covered slopes. The lower slopes of the Zagros Mountains are covered with patches of elm, maple, pistachio, and walnut trees. Willow and poplar grow in the ravines, as well as many creepers. Dense forests also abound on the slopes of the Elburz. Ash, cypress, elm, and oak trees are common there, together with some broadleaved evergreens, ferns, and shrubs.

Brown bears, wild goats and sheep, wolves, and leopards thrive in the remote mountains. Amphibians, such as frogs and salamanders, live around the fast-flowing streams on the lower slopes. Cat snakes, rat snakes, and vipers hunt in the undergrowth for lizards and small mammals.

▼ A mountain stream tumbles through a lush valley in the Elburz Mountains in northwestern Iran.

## Scrublands

Heading down the slopes toward the central plateau, the woodlands thin out and give way to patches of almond trees and bushes such as barberry and juniper.

A low shrub called sagebrush is common in grassy areas, while acacias, dwarf palms, and wormwood grow on drier land. The grasses and shrubs are home to many small animals. Most are rodents, such as hamsters and gerbils, as well as small hopping mice called jerboas. Larger animals in the area include deer, gazelles, rabbits, and hedgehogs. Hyenas, foxes, jackals, and sand boas are the plateau's hunters.

▲ The plain near Iran's border with Azerbaijan is too dry for trees. It receives only enough water for small shrubs to grow.

## DONKEY ON THE EDGE

The Persian onager is a wild relative of the domestic donkey. Because of its short legs, the onager (*pictured right*) cannot run as fast as a horse, but it can keep on the move for a long time. Onagers were used by the ancient Sumerians to pull chariots. They were once widespread in deserts from Israel to Afghanistan. Today there are fewer than 150 onagers in Iran. All of them live in two protected reserves.

▲ Iran's government has passed laws to protect the Persian onager. However, illegal hunting and competition for grazing and water with domestic livestock continue to threaten the onager with extinction.

Few species survive in Iran's deserts. Some isolated oases in the Kavir Desert support acacias, date palms, oleanders, plums, and tamarisk trees.

## Bird Stop

Many birds spend the whole winter on Iran's northern and southern coasts or around the country's lakes and inland wetlands. Other species use the country as a stopover as they travel to and from wintering areas in Africa or South Asia. Waterbirds such as seagulls, ducks, geese, and terns thrive on the shores of the Caspian Sea and the Persian Gulf. The wetlands around Lake Urmia are breeding areas for the greater flamingo, the great white pelican, and other species.

Many other bird species live in Iran all year round. Meat-eaters such as the bearded vulture and golden eagle make their homes in the high mountains. A few species, including the giant houbara bustard and desert warbler, scratch out a living in the dry plains.

## PURR-FECT PURR-SIANS

Iran is not only famous for big cats. The Persian cat is one of the oldest breeds of pet cats. These cats came from the high plateaus of Iran, where their long, silky fur protected them from the bitter cold. Italian traders brought the breed to Europe in the 17th century. The striking cats became popular with wealthy people as an exotic status symbol.

▲ Persian cats have round heads and short legs. They are sometimes referred to as longhairs.

## SEASONAL SEAL

The Caspian seal is the only mammal species to live in the Caspian Sea. Between the months of May and September, most seals are found in the deep, cool waters of the southern Caspian off the northern coast of Iran. In the fall, the seals head north to shallow waters that freeze over in winter. The seals breed and rear their pups on the ice.

In the summer of 2000, about 10,000 Caspian seals were found dead. They had been killed by an epidemic of canine distemper, a disease caused by a virus that normally affects dogs.

► This body of a Caspian seal washed up in 2000. Today, the population of seals has recovered well.

## Coastal Visitors

Iran is bordered by two seas, but they are very different from each other. The Persian Gulf—an arm of the Indian Ocean—contains 200 species of fish. Dolphins, porpoises, and whales are also found there, although their numbers are falling due to frequent oil spills.

The Caspian Sea is less salty than the ocean and is home to a different group of fish. They include large sturgeons, which were once common. Today, sturgeon are rare due to overfishing and poaching. The fish's salted eggs, called caviar, are in demand as a luxury food around the world.

▼ The dugong, a sea mammal related to manatees, is a rare visitor to the Persian Gulf.

# From Ancient
## Power
### to Religious
# Revolution

**I**RAN IS ONE OF THE OLDEST nations in the world. Its history dates back tens of thousands of years, although in the West it was called Persia rather than Iran until 1935. The land was the birthplace for some of the world's first civilizations. These slowly grew into the mighty Persian Empire, which ruled over the entire Greater Middle East and became the world's first superpower.

Iran has been at the center of many wars through its long history, and their effects can still be traced in the modern country. The invasion by Arab people in the seventh century has left its mark in particular by introducing the religion of Islam to Iran.

The Islamic Republic of Iran was born in 1979, when religious leaders toppled the monarchy.

◀ These 2,500-year-old carvings on the walls of Persepolis show representatives of peoples of the Persian Empire coming to pay their respects to the shah.

# ANCIENT CIVILIZATIONS

P eople were living in villages on the central plateau of Iran at least 10,000 years ago. These settlements grew into the great city of Susa, beginning the Proto-Elamite culture in 3200 B.C. The Elamites took over 500 years later. They often fought with Mesopotamia, their neighbor to the west, but they kept control of western Iran for 2,000 years. Aryans emerged in the east; they may have originated there. *Iran* means "land of the Aryans." Aryans called the Medes took over western Iran in the 8th century B.C. In 559 B.C., another group of Aryans, called the Persians, rose to power in the southwestern region of Fars. Under their leader Cyrus, the Persians defeated the Medes and created the Persian Empire.

 These walls are all that remains of Susa, one of the first cities ever built in Iran or anywhere else.

## Time line

This chart shows the approximate dates of the different cultures and rulers that have controlled Iran.

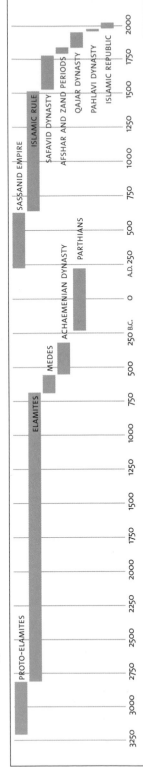

PROTO-ELAMITES

ELAMITES

MEDES

ACHAEMENIAN DYNASTY

PARTHIANS

SASSANID EMPIRE

ISLAMIC RULE

SAFAVID DYNASTY

AFSHAR AND ZAND PERIODS

QAJAR DYNASTY

PAHLAVI DYNASTY

ISLAMIC REPUBLIC

3350 3000 2750 2500 2250 2000 1750 1500 1250 1000 750 500 250 B.C. 0 A.D. 250 500 750 1000 1250 1500 1750 2000

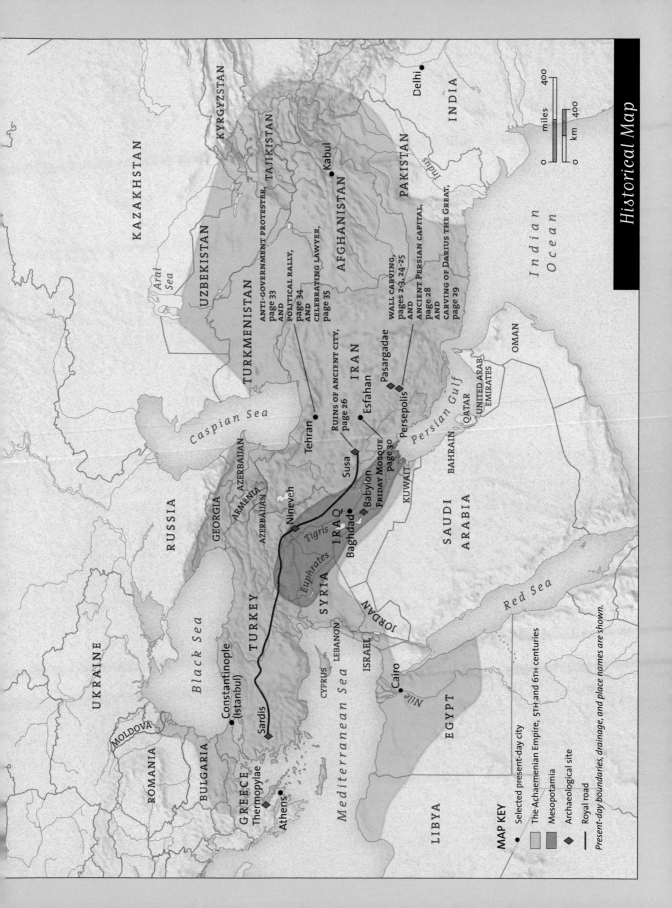

# Historical Map

KAZAKHSTAN

KYRGYZSTAN

UZBEKISTAN

TURKMENISTAN

TAJIKISTAN

Aral
Sea

RUSSIA

Caspian Sea

AFGHANISTAN

Kabul

ANTI-GOVERNMENT PROTESTER,
page 33
AND
POLITICAL RALLY,
page 34
AND
CELEBRATING LAWYER,
page 35

WALL CARVING,
pages 2–3, 24–25
AND
ANCIENT PERSIAN CAPITAL,
page 28
AND
CARVING OF DARIUS THE GREAT,
page 29

RUINS OF ANCIENT CITY,
page 26

IRAN

Tehran

PAKISTAN

Indus

Delhi

INDIA

GEORGIA

AZERBAIJAN

ARMENIA

AZERBAIJAN

Esfahan

Pasargadae

Persepolis

FRIDAY MOSQUE,
page 30

Susa

Nineveh

Tigris

Baghdad

IRAQ

Babylon

Euphrates

SYRIA

KUWAIT

Persian Gulf

BAHRAIN

QATAR

UNITED ARAB
EMIRATES

OMAN

Indian
Ocean

UKRAINE

MOLDOVA

ROMANIA

BULGARIA

Black Sea

TURKEY

Constantinople
(Istanbul)

Sardis

GREECE

Thermopylae

Athens

Mediterranean Sea

CYPRUS

LEBANON

ISRAEL

JORDAN

Cairo

Nile

EGYPT

LIBYA

Red Sea

SAUDI
ARABIA

SAUDI

## MAP KEY

- Selected present-day city
  The Achaemenian Empire, 5th and 6th centuries
  Mesopotamia
◆ Archaeological site
— Royal road

*Present-day boundaries, drainage, and place names are shown.*

0    miles    400

0    km    400

# Empires Rise and Fall

Iran had been home to different cultures for millennia when the Achaemenians came to power in the sixth century B.C. Their ruler, Cyrus I, expanded the territory under Persian control. He even defeated Mesopotamia (modern Iraq), which had formerly been the major power in the region. After Cyrus's death, his son Cambyses conquered another great ancient civilization: Egypt. After Cambyses died, one of his generals, Darius, took control of Persia in 522 B.C.

Darius transformed the Persian Empire into one of the most advanced civilizations on Earth. When Darius died in 486 B.C., Persia had conquered all of its enemies but one—Greece. The two empires clashed several times before Alexander the Great, a Greek-

▼ Persepolis was the capital of the Persian Empire. Its ruins are located in the modern province of Fars, which still retains the name of the homeland of Persia's greatest rulers.

## DARIUS THE GREAT

Darius the Great built a vast empire that stretched from the Mediterranean Sea to the Indus River in what is now Pakistan. Darius's skill as an administrator helped make his empire the most powerful the world had then known. He expanded Susa and built a new capital at Persepolis—then called the "richest city under the sun." Darius constructed a paved highway known as the Royal Road, which ran 1,500 miles (2,400 km) from Susa to the coast of the Mediterranean. He also improved trade by starting a postal system, standardizing weights, and minting coins. Some 2,300 years ahead of his time, the narrow canal he built from the Nile River to the Red Sea was a forerunner of the modern Suez Canal.

▶ A carving at Persepolis shows Darius being shaded by servants. His great height in the carving reflects his status.

Macedonian general, conquered Persia in 330 B.C. The Greeks ruled Persia for the next 70 years before they were overthrown in an uprising led by the Parni, nomads from the grasslands north of modern Iran.

## Parthian Power

The Parni kings ruled for five centuries, but Parthia, as their kingdom is known, was seldom peaceful. Greek and then Roman forces tried to take over parts of the kingdom. In the first century A.D., Parthia began to split into smaller states. Crippled by these divisions and its wars with Rome, the kingdom collapsed. Eventually, power fell into the hands of a Persian noble called Ardashir.

▲ The Friday Mosque in Esfahan was built in the eighth century. It is one of the most famous early Islamic monuments in Iran.

# Islamic Conquest

Crowned in A.D. 224 as *shah*, or "king of kings," Ardashir began 400 years of Sassanid rule. Zoroastrianism became the official religion, and arts and architecture blossomed. However, after centuries of fighting the Romans, Persia was weak. It was overrun by Arabs fighting in the name of a new religion—Islam. Persia became part of the Islamic empire in A.D. 642. The empire was ruled by the caliph, the spiritual head of Islam, from Baghdad in the west. Persian governors were left to manage their own affairs, however. Persian culture absorbed Islamic influences but continued to be exciting and dynamic.

## WE THREE KINGS

Little is known about where Zoroastrianism or its founder, the prophet Zoroaster, came from. The oldest written records of Zoroastrianism are from the 5th century B.C. The Greek historian Herodotus describes the Medes, who were the first people to rule the whole of Iran. One of the Median tribes, called the Magi, were powerful Zoroastrian priests. The most famous Magi are the Three Wise Men of the Christian Nativity story, who brought gifts to the newborn Jesus Christ. The 13th-century Italian explorer Marco Polo claimed to have visited the graves of the Three Wise Men in what is now Iran's capital, Tehran.

▲ The Magi, or Three Wise Men, came from the east by following a bright star, perhaps a comet or exploding star.

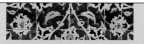

## CENTURIES OF SCHOLARS

Iran has a long history of scholarship. Under the Sassanids, the academy at Gondeshapur was a world center of medical knowledge. With the coming of Islam, Iran became home to many *nizamiyya*, where scholars studied and debated the meaning of Muslim scripture. In the Middle Ages, Iran attracted outstanding minds from throughout the Islamic world. They included Ibn Sina, called Avicenna in the West, who in the early 11th century wrote on subjects including philosophy and medicine. The 14 volumes of his *Canon of Medicine* served as the standard medical work throughout Europe for five centuries. Today, Iran is home to some of the most respected universities in the Greater Middle East: Some 2.2 million students study in more than 300 universities.

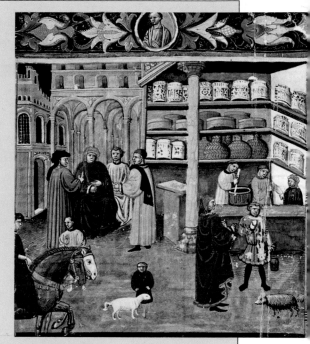

▲ This illustration comes from a 16th-century Italian edition of Ibn Sina's *Canon of Medicine*; it shows a physician and a druggist of the time.

In 1218, Persia was devastated by Mongols from East Asia. Persia was divided for the next 300 years, until Shah Ismail I reunited it as the Safavid Empire in 1501. By the start of the 17th century, Shah Abbas the Great had transformed Persia into a major power once again. By now most Persian people spoke Farsi and followed the Shiite branch of Islam.

## Outside Influence

Safavid rule ended when Mahmud Afghan from the east of the country invaded Esfahan, the capital, and

# NUMBERS INTO LETTERS

There is one thing that every math student can thank the Persians for—inventing algebra. Beginning in the seventh century, Persian mathematicians led the world. One scholar was Muhammad ibn Musa al-Khwarizmi, who set out a system using symbols to complete mathematical equations. The word *algebra* comes from part of the title of his book on the subject, *Kitab al-Jabr*. Later, Omar Khayyam became another celebrated mathematician and astronomer. His calculations helped reform the Persian calendar. Today, Khayyam is best remembered as the poet of the *Rubaiyat*, a long collection of four-line verses.

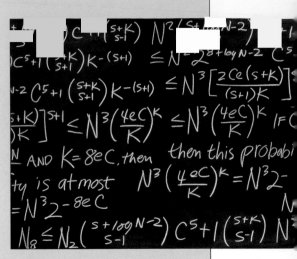

▲ Algebra uses letters to represent variables—numbers that can change.

▼ This woman was painted in the 1590s by Reza Abbasi, the leading Persian artist. Today, an art gallery in Tehran is named in his honor.

began a century of upheaval as various rulers took control. Finally, in 1796, Agha Mohammad Khan came to power and established the Qajar Dynasty.

Once again, Persia's important location in the region attracted the unwelcome attention of other powers. Persia lost part of its northern territory to Russia, while the British Empire took control of ports on the Persian Gulf. In return, Russia and Great Britain provided loans to Qajar rulers to help modernize Persia and strengthen its military forces. Western culture had increasing influence on Persian culture.

## The Coming of Change

Many Persians resented foreign control of their country. In 1906 they forced the Qajars to accept a new constitution and set up an elected parliament. Little changed, however.

Britain and Russia dominated Persian affairs during World War I (1914–1918). After the Russian Revolution in 1917, Britain was left in control of Persia, even though it officially claimed to support Iranian independence.

In 1921, Reza Khan, an army officer, seized power and adopted the name Pahlavi. He sought to reduce foreign influence and modernize the country. In 1935, he issue a royal decree that foreign diplomats should use the name Iran rather than Persia in their correspondence.

▲ Shah Mohammad Reza Pahlavi fled to the United States after he was overthrown in 1979.

## The Last Shah

When World War II broke out in 1939, Iran's ties with Germany alarmed the Soviet Union and Britain, which occupied Iran and forced the shah from power. His son, Shah Mohammad Reza, took the throne. The new shah fled in 1953, however, after clashing with Prime Minister Mohammad Mossadeq. U.S. agents started an uprising that overthrew Mossadeq, and the shah came back to the throne. He continued to modernize the country, making great improvements in public health. He was helped by the huge wealth created by the sale of oil.

▼ An Iranian shows his support for the Islamic movement against the shah in 1979.

Despite the economic success, many Iranians saw the monarchy as corrupt and immoral. They gathered around Ruhollah Khomeini, an ayatollah, or religious leader, who became the shah's main

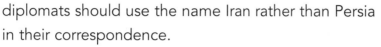

▲ An Iranian girl
carries a poster of
Ayatollah Khomeini
after a rally in Tehran in
2000 to celebrate the
anniversary of the
1979 revolution.

critic. In 1964, Khomeini was forced to leave the
country. Opposition to the shah continued, however.
He was overthrown in 1979, and the Islamic Revolution
became a success. Iran became an Islamic republic;
Khomeini returned as supreme leader.

## Neighbors at War

Khomeini's rule was dominated by tension with the
United States and war with Iraq. When the shah fled to
the United States, radical Iranians took 52 Americans
hostage at the U.S. embassy in Tehran. They held
them for over a year. Iran's relations with the United
States had been strong since World War II. Now, the
two countries stopped even talking to each other.

In 1980, Iraqi leader Saddam Hussein invaded Iran
to claim control of the Shatt al Arab and nearby oil
fields. Iranian forces recovered and pushed the Iraqis
back. The war lasted until 1988, when the United
Nations (UN) negotiated a ceasefire. A year later

Shirin Ebadi is one of Iran's leading campaigners for democracy and for increased rights for women and children. Born in 1947, Ebadi studied law at Tehran University before becoming Iran's first female judge. In the Islamic republic, however, women were not allowed to hold such posts. Ebadi was forced to resign in 1979. She started her own law practice and became famous for taking on human rights cases that often brought her into conflict with the conservative government and court system. Some of her clients were even murdered by intelligence agents. Ebadi herself has been briefly imprisoned and banned from practicing law. She has to move around in Iran with bodyguards. In 2003 she became the first Muslim woman and the first Iranian to be awarded the Nobel Peace Prize for her support of human rights without regard for her own safety.

▲ Shirin Ebadi (*center, in blue headscarf*) celebrates her Nobel prize during a visit to a home for street children she founded.

Khomeini died; Ayatollah Ali Khamenei became supreme leader.

## Liberal Changes

In 1997 new president Mohammad Khatami began reforms at home and proposed talks with other countries to resolve international tensions. At Iran's urging, the United Nations made 2001 "The Year of Dialogue Among Civilizations." After the terrorist attacks in the United States of September 11 that year, however, U.S. President George W. Bush labeled Iran part of an "axis of evil" that threatened world peace.

# Living in the
# *Islamic Republic*

**B**EFORE THE ISLAMIC REVOLUTION of 1979, Iran's culture had become widely influenced by the West. People watched Hollywood movies and listened to pop music. In the cities, many women wore Western clothes instead of the traditional black robe, or *chador*.

The revolutionary government rejected what it saw as immoral influences. Women covered up in public. Western pop music was banned. But in many ways traditional values did not change. Showing hospitality to guests is still important. Iranian music and poetry are as popular as ever. Strong religious beliefs have been part of the Iranian character for thousands of years. So has interaction with other cultures—both welcoming their influence and rejecting it.

◀ **Girls wearing chadors text their friends on a cell phone. Islamic traditions do not mean that all modern things are banned in Iran.**

# POPULATION GROWTH

There are about 70 million people in Iran. Most live in the big cities on the Central Plateau. The biggest city is the capital, Tehran, which is home to more than one sixth of all Iranians. Other large cities include Mashhad, Karaj, Esfahan, Tabriz, Shiraz, and Qom. All have populations of more than one million. By 2030, the United Nations predicts that more than 80 percent of Iranians will live in cities. In addition, Iran hosts around one million refugees, most of whom have come from war-torn Afghanistan and Iraq. Another 4 million Iranians live in Europe, North and South America, and Australia. Most moved abroad following the revolution of 1979.

| 1950 / 17 million | 1970 / 29 million |
|---|---|
| 27% urban / 73% rural | 42% urban / 58% rural |

| 1990 / 57 million | 2005 / 70 million |
|---|---|
| 56% urban / 44% rural | 68% urban / 32% rural |

▶ **Life in Iran's cities offers all sorts of fun activities—like shopping for cosmetics.**

## Common Iranian Phrases

Iranians speak a language called Farsi. Farsi is usually written in the Arabic alphabet. Here are a few Farsi words and phrases. Give them a try:

| | |
|---|---|
| Hello | Sah-laam |
| Goodbye | Kho-dah ha-fez |
| Please | Khaw-hesh me-conan |
| Thank you | Tah-shah-core |
| Yes | Baa-lay |
| No | Kheyr |
| How are you? | Hal-e shoma che towreh |

## Population Map

### MAP KEY

**Population of urban area**

- ◼ Over 5 million
- ▲ 1 million to 5 million
- ● 500,000 to 1 million
- • Under 500,000

**People per square kilometer**

**People per square mile**

| People per square mile | People per square kilometer |
|---|---|
| More than 2500 | More than 1000 |
| 1250–2499 | 500–999 |
| 250–1249 | 100–499 |
| 25–249 | 10–99 |
| 2.5–24 | 1–9 |
| Less than 2.5 | Less than 1 |

TURKEY

ARMENIA

AZERBAIJAN

AZERBAIJAN

TURKMENISTAN

AFGHANISTAN

PAKISTAN

IRAQ

KUWAIT

SAUDI ARABIA

BAHRAIN

QATAR

UNITED ARAB EMIRATES

OMAN

*Caspian Sea*

*Persian Gulf*

*Gulf of Oman*

*Strait of Hormuz*

Orūmīyeh (Urmia)

Tabrīz

Ardabīl

Būkān

Zanjān

Rasht

Sanandaj

Qazvīn

Hamadān

Kermānshāh

Borūjerd

Khorramābād

Arāk

Eslamshahr

Karaj

Tehrān

Qom

Bābol

Sārī

Gorgān

Bojnūrd

Sabzevār

Neyshābūr

Mashhad

Āhvāz

Khorramshahr

Ābādān

Khomeynīshahr

Najafābād

Eşfahān (Isfahan)

Yazd

Birjand

Zāhedān

Kermān

Sīrjān

Shīrāz

Bandar-e 'Abbās

**GIRLS SENDING MESSAGE,** pages 3, 36-37 **AND**

**PRAYING SOLDIERS IN NATIONAL COLORS,** page 40 **AND**

**GIRLS IN RESTAURANT,** page 41

**FRIDAY PRAYERS,** page 41

**CARPETMAKING,** page 46

**WOMEN SHOPPING** page 38

miles 0 200

km 0 200

## Putting Religion First

Almost all Iranians are Muslims, and 90 percent of them follow the Shia branch of Islam. That makes Iran an unusual country. Most Islamic countries and Muslims worldwide follow the Sunni branch—as do about 6 percent of Iranians. From everyday life to the national government, Islam is central to Iranian society.

*Namaz (Salat)* is a prayer Muslims must perform five times every day. Most people gather at mosques, but the prayer can also be said by individuals. Prayers dictate the routine of the entire day. They are said at dawn, midday, mid-afternoon, sunset, and at nightfall.

Like other Muslims, Iranians fast (do not eat or drink) during daylight hours in the month of Ramadan

▼ Soldiers from the Iranian Army wear red, white, and green to create the pattern of the Iranian flag while they pray in 2006.

in the Islamic calendar. For this purpose, people wake before sunrise to have breakfast and then wait until sunset to eat their evening meal.

The next largest religious group are Christians, followed by Zoroastrians, whose religion began in ancient Persia.

▲ Friday prayers take place in the new extension of the Holy Shrine of Hazrat e Masoomeh in Qom.

## Iranian Cuisine

Muslims are forbidden to eat pork. Pigs are considered to be unclean animals, unfit for consumption. Muslims do eat some meat, mostly lamb, but the animal must be killed in a certain way and a prayer must be said before the slaughter.

A typical Iranian family meal consists of chicken, beef, or fish cooked with vegetables and fresh herbs and served with rice and side dishes of cheese, cucumber, tomatoes, onions, and yogurt. Iranians eat flat bread, called *nan-e lavash*, with every meal. Other Iranian dishes include *kookoo*, a pie filled with meat and vegetables, and *aash*, a thick soup. A stew called *khoresht-e fesenjan*, made with chicken or duck, pomegranate juice, and ground walnuts, is an old Persian dish that is still popular today.

▼ A pizza parlor in Tehran is one of the few places where young men and women can socialize.

## FROM THE GRILL

Chelow kebab and joojeh kebab are two Iranian national dishes and the fast-food equivalent of burgers. Chelow kebabs consist of grilled meat—lamb or beef—and steamed saffron rice. The traditional drink with chelow kebab is *doogh*—yogurt mixed with fizzy mineral water and flavored with salt and mint. Joojeh kebabs consist of grilled chicken served with potatoes and cooked vegetables or sometimes with rice. Western-style fast food is popular among young Iranians, although it is often prepared differently and served alongside traditional dishes.

▲ A chicken joojeh kebab

▼ This water jug was used to wash before eating with the fingers.

# Wedding Days

Modern Iranian weddings combine Islamic and ancient Persian traditions. There are two stages to a marriage: The first stage is called *Aghd*, which is the most formal part of the ceremony. This takes place in a room decorated with flowers. A ceremonial rug called the *Sofreh-ye Aghd* covers the floor. The rug is made of a luxurious fabric such as cashmere or silk. It faces east in the direction of the sunrise. Symbolic items, such as spices, a mirror, and candles, are placed on the Sofreh-ye Aghd to bless the marriage.

The bride dresses in white, the groom in black. The bride is asked three times if she consents to marriage; she remains silent twice but accepts on the third time. The signing of the wedding contract marks the end of the ceremony. The couple then exchange rings and feed each other honey to sweeten their marriage.

The second stage is a celebration, called *Jashn-e Aroosi*. Most couples choose to have a big party with food and dancing. Traditionally, Iranian weddings are very expensive. The government pays for mass weddings to reduce the cost and encourage young Iranians to get married.

# An Ancient Art Scene

Iranian arts and architecture owe much to the country's rich history. Iran boasts some of the world's greatest historical monuments, such as the remains of the great hall in the royal palace built by Darius at Persepolis.

The Islamic conquest also left a lasting mark on Persian architecture such as Imam Mosque in Esfahan. The mosque combines both Islamic and Persian influences. Other Persian arts also flourished after the arrival of Islam, most notably literature. Iran's greatest poet was Ferdowsi, who wrote in the 10th century. He wrote in Farsi, even though Arabic was the language of Iran's rulers. Ferdowsi's masterpiece, *Shahnameh*

## PUBLIC HOLIDAYS

Iran has a unique calendar that dates back to the 11th century. It begins on the spring equinox—when the day and night are the same length—based on precise astronomic observations from Tehran, which make it highly accurate. The numbering of years starts from the *hejrah*, or journey, of the Prophet Mohammad from Mecca to Medina, which according to the Western calendar took place in A.D. 622. The names of the Iranian months come from the Zoroastrian calendar. Iran has two kinds of holidays: religious holidays based on the 354-day Islamic calendar and national holidays based on the Iranian calendar. The national holidays are:

| | |
|---|---|
| FARVARDIN 1–4 | Iranian New Year |
| FARVARDIN 12 | Islamic Republic Day |
| FARVARDIN 13 | Sizdah Bedar (Nature Day) |
| BAHMAN 22 | Islamic Revolution Day |
| KHURDAD 14 | Anniversary of the death of Ayatollah Khomeini |

## NEW YEAR IRANIAN STYLE

O n March 21 (FARVARDIN 1), Iranians celebrate Norouz—the Iranian New Year. People prepare by cleaning their homes and buying new clothes. On the last Wednesday before Norouz, Iranians ensure good luck for the coming year by jumping over bonfires.

Norouz lasts for 13 days, during which time people visit their family and friends and eat meals at a table covered with seven items starting with the letter "s"—a tradition known as *Haft Seen*. The last day of the Norouz is called *Sizdah Bedar*, or Nature Day. On this day, everyone celebrates outside with family picnics, music, and dancing.

▲ Iranian-American dancers put on a colorful performance in New York City during Norouz celebrations.

(The Epic of Kings), is the national poem of Iran. It continues to influence contemporary Iranian literature.

Iran has unique traditions of classical and folk music. Folk instruments such as the *tanbur*, a long-necked lute, are rarely played anywhere else. Ethnic groups such as the Azerbaijanis also have their own music and styles of dance, which are performed in colorful costumes. Today, Iranian pop artists such as Arian and O-Hum are very popular.

## The Arts Since the Revolution

Since the Islamic revolution of 1979, artistic expression has been subject to state approval. Most newspapers and all television and radio networks are run by the government. Books and films are checked to ensure that they do not contain anti-government ideas. Many artists and writers have moved abroad, but others have still been able to create thoughtful works within Iran. Iranians have also found a new voice in the post-revolutionary era. Many Iranians have access to the outside world through the Internet. Some have started blogs about their lives. Religious leaders in Iran have become wary of the Internet, and bloggers are now required to register with the government.

## ON THE BIG SCREEN

Movies are very popular in Iran. Although the government controls what can be shown, it also contributes toward the cost of making movies. One of the most famous Iranian directors is Abbas Kiarostami, who made *Close-Up* in 1990. The movie blurs fact and fiction when a man impersonates a famous real-life Iranian director. One of the most famous Iranian movies abroad is *Children of Heaven*, made in 1998 by the director Majid Majidi. The comedy tells the story of a boy from a poor family who loses his little sister's shoes. He enters a race to try to win her a new pair of shoes so that she can go to school. The movie was nominated for the Best Foreign Language Film at the Academy Awards.

◀ *Children of Heaven* was produced by the Institute for the Intellectual Development of Children, funded by the Iranian government.

# All Sorts of Sports

Iran has a lot of young people, and many of them play sports in their spare time. Women play non-contact sports, such as volleyball, and racket sports such as badminton. Strength sports and martial arts are popular among men. Wrestling is Iran's national sport, and Iranian athletes regularly achieve success in world championships and the Olympics. Weightlifting is another popular sport thanks to the "Iranian Hercules," Hossein Reza Zadeh, who holds world

## ON THE CARPET

As long ago as 529 B.C., it was said that the tomb of King Cyrus was covered in precious carpets. Over two thousand years later, the 16th century Safavid king Shah Abbas set up a royal workshop where weavers made high quality carpets of silk with gold and silver thread. Persian carpets are still the best in the world. Weavers use tiny knots of wool or silk to create flowers, animals, or shapes. Fine carpets might have 330 knots in a square inch. A skilled weaver can tie up to 12,000 knots a day. In 2007, Iran produced the world's largest handmade carpet for a mosque in the United Arab Emirates: It was the size of a soccer field, and

▲ A woman makes a carpet in Isfahan. Iranian cities have their own styles of weaving, so experts can tell where a carpet was made.

took 1,200 weavers 18 months to make in nine separate segments. The carpet used so much wool that some had to be imported from New Zealand.

## SPORT OF KINGS

Polo is a sport with a long history. The exact origins of the game are unknown, but records show that it was being played in Persia as early as the 6th century B.C. At this time, polo was used as training for the cavalry.

In the 17th century, Shah Square in Esfahan was built as a polo field by Shah Abbas I for members of his household and family. Polo became the Persian national sport and spread throughout Asia. Today the game is also played in Argentina, Brazil, and Great Britain, where it is popular with the royal family. Even now, polo is still a "sport of kings."

▲ A polo match in a detail from a Persian miniature painting of the 16th century

records in the sport's super heavyweight class. Iran's mountains offer a range of opportunities for sports, such as climbing, hiking, and skiing. Games like chess and backgammon are popular in teahouses.

By far the most popular spectator sport in Iran is soccer. The national team has won the Asian Cup three times and played in three World Cup Final competitions. Iran has a successful professional soccer league and several Iranians play for leading European teams.

◀ Hossein Reza Zadeh wins a gold medal for weightlifting at the 2004 Olympics in Athens. He also holds the world record and is a big star in Iran. His wedding was shown live on Iranian TV.

# Religion
## and
# Reform

I RAN WAS TRANSFORMED WHEN Ayatollah Khomeini came to power. The new constitution introduced Islamic laws, or *sharia*. Anyone who criticized the government was locked up or even executed. Khomeini promised to improve the lives of all Iranians, but the economy collapsed as skilled workers fled and Iran fought a long war with Iraq.

That war is over now, and Iran's Islamic rule is no longer new. The laws have not changed, but they are not applied so strictly and the economy is in better shape. Iran still faces one big problem, however. Some other countries believe that it is developing nuclear weapons. Iran insists that it has cooperated with United Nations inspectors checking its nuclear facilities, but the conflict has isolated the country again.

◄Western pop music is banned in Iran, but many Iranians are familiar with Western musicians. Persian pop music is widely available in music stores like this one in Tehran.

At a Glance

# LOCAL GOVERNMENT

Iran is an Islamic republic made up of 30 provinces, or *ostanha*. Some of the provinces have names that date back thousands of years, but others have been created in the last decades. Highly populated areas are divided into numerous small provinces, but in areas where there are relatively few people, provinces can be very large. Each province has a governor, appointed by the council of ministers after being proposed by the minister of interior affairs, and a council elected by popular vote. There are also city, district, and village councils to which members are elected for four-year terms. Many women have been elected to such bodies, giving them a influential voice in local affairs. Local councils echo a long tradition in Iran of cooperative action among members of communities.

▼ **Five of the most powerful men in Iran, from left to right: the leader of the Guardian Council, head of the Assembly of Experts, two former presidents, and the supreme leader** (*on a chair*).

# Trading Partners

Iran's economy has been hit hard by a trade ban imposed by the United States since 1979. The situation was worsened because some countries believed Iran was developing nuclear facilities. In 2006, those nations imposed sanctions. After economic success at the beginning of the century, Iranians are now finding it hard to make ends meet. The country's unrefined oil and natural gas contribute to around 85 percent of exports. Imports include food, medicine, refined gasoline, and military and manufactured goods.

| Country | Percentage Iran exports |
|---|---|
| Japan | 16.9% |
| China | 11.2% |
| Italy | 6.0% |
| South Korea | 5.8% |
| All others combined | 60.1% |

| Country | Percentage Iran imports |
|---|---|
| Germany | 13.9% |
| United Arab Emirates | 8.4% |
| China | 8.3% |
| Italy | 7.1% |
| All others combined | 62.3% |

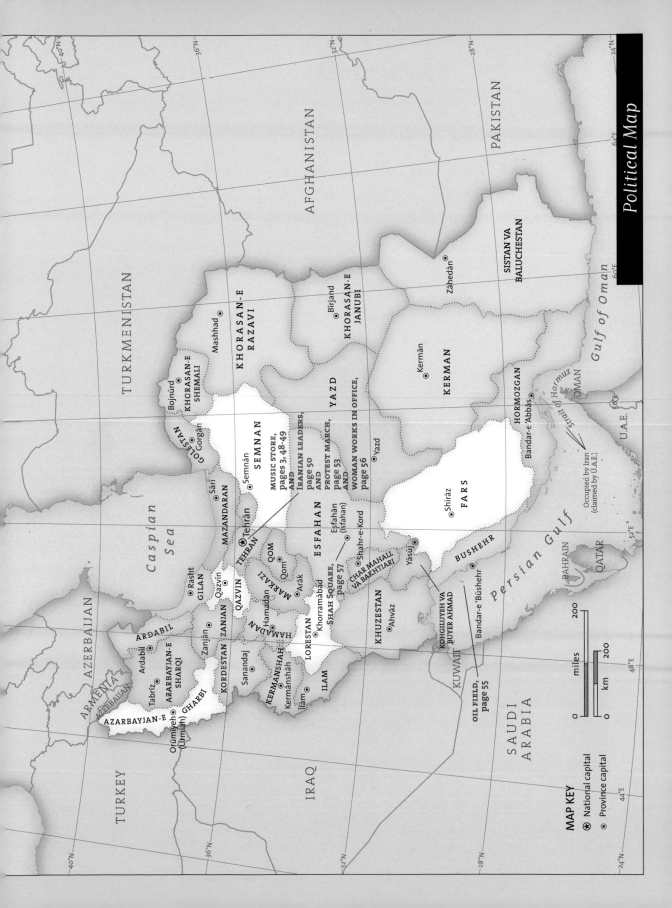

Political Map

TURKEY

ARMENIA

AZERBAIJAN

AZERBAIJAN

TURKMENISTAN

AFGHANISTAN

PAKISTAN

Caspian
Sea

AZARBAYJAN-E
GHARBI

Orūmīyeh
(Urmiah)

Tabrīz

Ardabīl

ARDABIL

AZARBAYJAN-E
SHARQI

Zanjān

KORDESTAN

Sanandaj

ZANJAN

GILAN

Rasht

Qazvīn

QAZVIN

Sārī

Bojnūrd

Gorgān

GOLESTAN

KHORASAN-E
SHEMALI

Mashhad

KHORASAN-E
RAZAVI

MAZANDARAN

Semnān

SEMNAN

TEHRAN

Tehrān

MUSIC STORE,
pages 3, 48-49
AND
IRANIAN LEADERS,
page 50
AND
PROTEST MARCH,
page 53
AND
WOMAN WORKS IN OFFICE,
page 56

Birjand

KHORASAN-E
JANUBI

Zāhedān

SISTAN VA
BALUCHESTAN

QOM

Qom

MARKAZI

Hamadān

Arāk

HAMADAN

KERMANSHAH

Kermānshāh

Khorramābād

LORESTAN

ESFAHAN

Eşfahān
(Işfahān)

SHAH SQUARE,
page 57

Shahr-e-Kord

CHAR MAHALL
VA BAKHTIARI

YAZD

Yazd

Kermān

KERMAN

HORMOZGAN

Bandar-e 'Abbās

Strait of Hormuz

OMAN

Gulf of Oman

60°E

ĪlāmĪLAM

Ahvāz

KHUZESTAN

Yāsūj

Shīrāz

FARS

Vāsūj

KOHGILUYEH VA
BUYER AHMAD

BUSHEHR

Bandar-e 'Būshehr

OIL FIELD,
page 55

Persian Gulf

KUWAIT

SAUDI
ARABIA

BAHRAIN

QATAR

U.A.E.

Occupied by Iran
(claimed by U.A.E.)

IRAQ

MAP KEY

⊛ National capital
⦿ Province capital

0       200
miles

0       200
km

# A New Republic

The supreme leader of Iran wields ultimate political power. In 1979, Ayatollah Khomeini formed a system of government that would create laws that agreed with Islamic traditions. At that time the politics of Iran was dominated by the Islamic Revolutionary Party, which favored a strictly controlled society. When the Islamic Revolutionary Party broke up in 1987 and Ayatollah Khomeini died two years later, various political groups began to appear. Most of them supported the ideas of the Islamic Revolution, but a few now call for greater social and political freedoms.

## HOW THE GOVERNMENT WORKS

Ayatollah Ali Khamenei became supreme leader following the death of Ayatollah Khomeini. Khamenei was appointed by the Assembly of Experts. The Experts are religious leaders who are elected by the public every four years. Khamenei will serve until his death but could be dismissed by the Experts at any time. As the supreme leader, he controls the military, courts, and state television and radio networks. He also appoints the Expediency Council, a team of powerful advisors. The president is elected by the people every four years. He is Iran's second-in-command and is served by a Council of Ministers and a number of vice-presidents. The elected parliament, or Majlis, elects its own head of parliament. All elected officials in Iran must be approved first by the Council of Guardians.

| SUPREME LEADER | | |
|---|---|---|
| EXECUTIVE | LEGISLATIVE | JUDICIARY |
| PRESIDENT | HEAD OF PARLIAMENT | HEAD OF JUDICIARY |
| COUNCIL OF MINISTERS | MAJILIS (290 MEMBERS) | SUPREME COURT |

## Slow Reform

By the late 1990s, the political situation began to change. In 1997, a reformer called Mohammed Khatami was elected as Iran's president. In the parliamentary elections of 2000, candidates who wanted reform were more popular than the conservatives. However, despite winning many seats in the parliament, the liberal politicians were opposed by the supreme leader, Ayatollah Khamenei. As a result, the parliament could not do anything to make life better for the people who voted for it.

## GUARDIANS AT WORK

The Guardian Council is one of the most powerful of all of Iran's governing bodies. None of its 12 members are elected. Instead, the supreme leader makes six religious leaders members of the Council. The remaining six places are filled by lawyers whose appointments are approved by the Majilis. The council ensures that new laws conform to Islamic law and Iran's constitution. It also manages elections and can stop people from running as candidates. In the 2005 presidential race, the Guardians banned most of the candidates from running for office. The council also controls who gets to run for election to the Assembly of Experts—the governing body that chooses the supreme leader.

▼ Demonstrations against the government are rare. However, Iranians often protest about foreign countries.

# INDUSTRY MAP

This map shows the location of Iran's industrial centers. Most of Iran's industry is involved in the export of crude oil and natural gas. Despite having large reserves of crude oil, Iran has few refineries and has to import a lot of its gasoline and other fuels.

**MAP KEY**
- ⚙ Manufacturing center
- ⛏ Coal mining
- ♨ Natural gas
- 🛢 Petroleum
- ⛽ Petroleum refinery
- ⚗ Petrochemicals

▶ **President Ahmadinejad holds a press conference. The Iranian president's sometimes controversial views mean that people throughout the region want to know what he has to say.**

The conservatives took back control of the government in 2004. Any hopes of reform suffered in 2005, when Mahmoud Ahmadinejad, a close supporter of the supreme leader, became the new president. Just a few months into the job, Ahmadinejad sparked an international outcry with his outspoken attacks on Israel.

## Black Gold

Iran's economy was in ruins when the bloody war with Iraq ended in 1988. During the war, Iraq had bombed cities and villages, and Iran's roads and water supplies were destroyed. The total damage was estimated at $1 trillion. The task of rebuilding Iran was further hampered by trade restrictions imposed by the United States.

However, Iran has one thing on its side:

Vast oil wealth. Iran has the third-largest reserves of crude oil in the world and the second-largest reserves of natural gas. That means the country can still attract billions of dollars of foreign investment, despite the U.S. trade restrictions. So much money comes from places such as Brazil, China, Japan, and many European countries, that oil and natural gas generate more than half of Iran's wealth.

## GREATER PERSIA

Iranian people do not live just in Iran. People who speak Farsi and related languages are found throughout Central Asia in a region described by Iran's leaders as the Iranian Cultural Continent. Historically, this covers the land occupied by Persians at the height of their empire. It extends from India and Uzbekistan in the east to the Caucasus Mountains in the north and west to Syria and Turkey.

## *Building the Economy*

Iran's reserves of oil and natural gas will not last forever. As a result, the Iranian government is investing in other industries to help build the economy. It has built dams and set up irrigation projects to help farmers grow valuable foods such as dates, pistachios,

▼ A tanker takes on a load of oil at the Kharg Island oil field off the coast of Iran in the Persian Gulf.

and saffron, which can be sold abroad. Iran also produces a wide range of manufactured goods such as cars, electronics, textiles, and chemicals and drugs made from oil. Iran is also the best place to buy a carpet or *kilim*, a traditional handwoven Persian rug.

## WOMEN IN IRAN

The role of women in Iran has changed since the early years of the 20th century. Traditionally, Iranian women stayed at home and looked after their children. In public, they wore the chador, or veil, as part of the Islamic dress code of *hijab*, or "modesty." In 1936, the shah banned women from wearing the chador in an attempt to modernize Iran. Some women began to wear Western-style clothes, which angered religious leaders. Despite these changes, most women continued in their traditional domestic roles. The Islamic Revolution changed all that. Although hijab became mandatory again, the new constitution allowed women to take an active role in public life. Today, more women go to college than men. Many women have careers before they have children. It is a long way from equality, but women enjoy far greater freedom than ever before.

▲ A woman at work in Tehran's stock exchange

## *Visit the Past*

Tourism is another growing industry in modern Iran. Few foreigners dared to visit Iran in the years of war after the 1979 revolution. But the country's rich history and natural beauty are once more starting to attract visitors.

The government is encouraging tourists. It has made it much easier to get a visa that allows travelers to visit Iran, and has invested in roads, railroads, and airports. Most tourists are Muslims from Asian countries. They make pilgrimages to the religious shrines in Mashhad and Qom. Iran is also becoming a more popular destination among Western tourists who visit historical sites such as Persepolis.

Iran's tense relations with the West, however, make the future of such tourism uncertain, along with the future of the country. Many other nations are nervous about Iran's aims. As in its past, Iran may become somewhat isolated from much of the rest of the world. As history shows, however, Iran's key location in the Greater Middle East guarantees that it will not be long before it is once again at the very heart of international affairs.

▼ Horse-drawn carriages wait to carry tourists around Shah Square in Esfahan. The square, built in the early 17th century, is one of the largest in the world.

# Add a Little Extra to Your Country Report!

I f you are assigned to write a report about Iran, you'll want to include basic information about the country, of course. The Fast Facts chart on page 8 will give you a good start. The rest of the book will give you the details you need to create a full and up-to-date paper or PowerPoint presentation. But what can you do to make your report more fun than anyone else's? If you use your imagination and dig a bit deeper into some of the topics introduced in this book, you're sure to come up with information that will make your report unique!

## >Flag

Perhaps you could explain the history of Iran's flag, and the meanings of its colors and symbol. Go to **www.crwflags.com/fotw/flags** for more information.

## >National Anthem

How about downloading Iran's national anthem, and playing it for your class? At **www.nationalanthems.info** you'll find what you need, including the words to the anthem, plus sheet music for it. Simply pick "I" and then "Iran" from the list on the left-hand side of the screen, and you're on your way.

## >Time Difference

If you want to understand the time difference between Iran and where you are, this Web site can help: **www.worldtimeserver.com**. Just pick "Iran" from the list on the left. If you called someone in Iran right now, would you wake them up from their sleep?

## >Currency

Another Web site will convert your money into rials, the currency used in Iran. You'll want to know how much money to bring if you're ever lucky enough to travel to Iran: **www.xe.com/ucc**.

## >Weather

Why not check the current weather in Iran? It's easy—go to **www.weather.com** to find out if it's sunny or cloudy, warm or cold in Iran right now! Pick "World" from the headings at the top of the page. Then search for Iran. Click on any city. Be sure to click on the tabs below the weather report for Sunrise/Sunset information, Weather Watch, and Business Travel Outlook, too. Scroll down the page for the 36-hour Forecast and a satellite weather map. Compare your weather to the weather in the Iranian city you chose. Is this a good season, weather-wise, for a person to travel to Iran?

## >Miscellaneous

Still want more information? Go to National Geographic's World Atlas for Young Explorers site at **http://www.nationalgeographic.com/kids-world-atlas**. It will help you find maps, photos, music, games, and other features that you can use to jazz up your report.

# Glossary

**Arab** a person whose distant ancestors come from the Arabian Peninsula in southwest Asia.

**Archaeologist** a scientist who studies the remains of ancient people to learn more about how people lived in the past.

**Caliph** the leader of an early Islamic empire.

**Cavalry** troops mounted on horseback.

**Ceasefire** an agreement between two nations at war to stop fighting.

**Circa** about; used to indicate a date that is approximate, and abbreviated as ca.

**Climate** the average weather of a certain place at different times of year.

**Conservative** a member or supporter of a traditional form of government.

**Culture** a collection of beliefs, traditions, and styles that belongs to people living in a certain part of the world.

**Economy** the system by which a country creates wealth through making and trading in products.

**Ecosystem** a community of living things and the environment they interact with; an ecosystem includes plants, animals, soil, water, and air.

**Empire** territories located in several parts of the world that are controlled by a single nation.

**Ethnic group** a large section of a country's population with members that share a common ancestry or background.

**Exported** transported and sold outside the country of origin.

**Extinct** when no members of a species are left alive.

**Imported** brought into the country from abroad.

**Liberal** a member or supporter of a form of government which supports individual's rights.

**Millennium** a period of one thousand years, or ten centuries; plural millennia.

**Mint** to make coins.

**Monarchy** a system of government that is headed by a king or queen.

**Mosque** a Muslim place of worship.

**Nativity** the story of the birth of Jesus Christ that is told at Christmas by Christians.

**Nomad** a person who moves from place to place rather than living in one location.

**Parliamentary** a system of government made up of a cabinet whose members belong to and are responsible to the governing body.

**Persian** the historical name for a person from Iran.

**Petroleum** oil and gas that is pumped up from beneath the surface of the Earth. Petroleum is refined to make gasoline and other fuels and provides the raw materials for plastics.

**Refugee** someone who is forced to leave their home to escape war or persecution and to seek refuge in a safer place.

**Sanctions** actions taken to enforce a law or rule.

**Species** a type of organism; animals or plants in the same species look similar and can only breed successfully among themselves.

# Bibliography

Fast, April. *Iran, The Land*. New York, NY: Crabtree Publishing, 2005.

Taus-Bolstad, Stacy. *Iran in Pictures*. Minneapolis, MN: Lerner Publications, 2004.

Walsh, Kieran. *Iran*. Vero Beach, FL: Rourke Publishing, 2004.

http://news.bbc.co.uk/1/shared/spl/hi/middle_east/06/iran_maps/html/default.stm (general information)

http://www.iranmiras.ir/en_site/Home_E.asp (cultural information)

# Further Information

## NATIONAL GEOGRAPHIC Articles

Mairson, Alan. "Desert Reptiles of Iran." NATIONAL GEOGRAPHIC (October 2004): 106–109.

Salak, Kira. "Travels in Hostile Territory." NATIONAL GEOGRAPHIC ADVENTURE (November 2006): 64–72, 105–106.

## Web sites to explore

More fast facts about Iran, from the CIA (Central Intelligence Agency): https://www.cia.gov/library/publications/the-world-factbook/geos/ir.html

Iran's political system is very complicated with several elected bodies and religious groups working together. Who is in charge? This graphic will help you unravel the jumble: http://news.bbc.co.uk/1/shared/spl/hi/middle_east/03/iran_power/html/default.stm

Find out more about Iran with the *Encyclopedia Iranica*, which contains articles on everything from Architecture to Zoroastrianism: http://www.iranica.com/newsite/

## See, hear

There are many ways to get a taste of life in Iran, such as movies, music, magazines, or TV shows. You might be able to locate these:

*Children of Heaven* (1997)
A comedy about a brother and sister growing up in Iran. When one of their pairs of shoes is stolen, the children begin a series of funny adventures to get the shoes back.

*Close Up* (1990)
A ground-breaking Iranian film that blurs the boundary between a movie and a documentary. It tells the true story of a man who pretended to be a famous movie director. The film includes footage of his real-life trial. At the end of the trial, the man meets the real director.

*Persepolis* (2003)
This illustrated novel was written by Marjane Satrapi. It describes her life growing up in Iran after the revolution of 1979. In 2007 *Persepolis* was made into an award-winning animated movie.

*Tehran Times*
Take a look at the news making headlines in Iran on the Web site of the *Tehran Times*, one of Iran's largest English-language newspapers: http://www.tehrantimes.com/

# Index

# Credits

## Picture Credits

Front Cover – Spine: Javarman/Shutterstock; Top: W. A. Rogers/NGIC; Low Far Left: James L. Stanfield/NGIC; Low Left: James P. Blair/NGIC; Low Right: Martin Gray/NGIC; Low Far Right: Alexander Avakain/NGIC.

Interior – Ahman A. Ali: 5 up, 41 up; Corbis: Archivo Iconografico, S. A.: 31 up; Dave Bartruff: 13 lo, 42 lo, 42 lo, 57 lo; Bettmann: 33up; Christophe Boisvieux: 46 up; Elio Ciol: 30 lo; Andrea Comas/Reuters: 47 up; Dean Conger: 10 up; Raheb Homavandi/Reuters: 3 left, 36-37, 50 lo; Maryan J./Perisan Eye: 38 up; Steve Kaufman: 2 right, 16-17, 21 lo; Jamal Nasrallah/epa: 14 lo; Steven Mark Needham/Envision: 57 up; Morteza Nikoubazi/ Reuters: 3 right, 11 up, 48-49; James Noble: 32 up; Micheline Peltetier: 35 up; Ryan Pyle: 13 up; Reuters: 23 lo, 34 up; Mohsen Shandiz: 11 lo; Smithsonian Institution: 32 lo; Sygma: 45 lo; Abedin Taherkenareh/epa: 40 lo, 42 up, 54 lo; Ramin Talaie: 44 up; Werner Forman 47 lo; Roger Wood: 26 up, 30 up; NGIC: Alexander Avakain: TP, 41 lo, 56 lo; James P. Blair: 15 up; Michael Coyne: 2 left, 6-7, 33 lo, 53 lo; Bruce Dale: 12 up, 21 up; David Doubilet: 23 up; Bobby Model: 20 center; W. A. Rogers: 55 lo; James L. Stanfield: 2-3, 24-25, 28 lo, 29 up; Raul Touzon: 22 up; Michael S. Yamashita: 14 up; NHPA: Tom Ang: 18 up; Shutterstock: Matt Trommer: 59 up.

For more information, please call 1-800-NGS-LINE (647-5463) or write to the following address:

NATIONAL GEOGRAPHIC SOCIETY
1145 17th Street N.W.
Washington, D.C. 20036-4688 U.S.A.

Visit the Society's Web site at
www.nationalgeographic.com/books

Library of Congress Cataloging-in-Publication Data available on request
ISBN: 978-1-4263-0200-8

Printed in the United States of America

Series design by Jim Hiscott.
The body text is set in Avenir; Knockout.
The display text is set in Matrix Script.

Front Cover—Top: Outdoor rug laundry, Shisma Ali, Tehran; Low Far Left: Relief sculpture, Persepolis; Low Left: Poppies; Low Right: Students at Basiri, southeast of Shiraz; Low Far Right: Ancient city of Bam

Page 1—Carpet weavers in Esfahan; Icon image on spine, Contents page, and throughout: Islamic tilework

## Produced through the worldwide resources of the National Geographic Society

John M. Fahey, Jr., *President and Chief Executive Officer*; Gilbert M. Grosvenor, *Chairman of the Board*; Nina D. Hoffman, *Executive Vice President, President of Book Publishing Group*

### National Geographic Staff for this Book

Nancy Laties Feresten, *Vice President, Editor-in-Chief of Children's Books*
Bea Jackson, *Director of Design and Illustration*
Jim Hiscott, *Art Director*
Priyanka Lamichhane, *Project Editor*
Lori Epstein, *Illustrations Editor*
Stacy Gold, Nadia Hughes, *Illustrations Research Editors*
R. Gary Colbert, *Production Director*
Lewis R. Bassford, *Production Manager*
Maryclare Tracy, Nicole Elliott, *Manufacturing Managers*
Maps, *Mapping Specialists, Ltd.*

### Brown Reference Group plc. Staff for this Book

*Volume Editor: Tom Jackson*
*Designer: Dave Allen*
*Picture Manager: Clare Newman*
*Maps: Martin Darlison, Encompass Graphics*
*Artwork: Darren Awuah*
*Index: Kay Ollerenshaw*
*Senior Managing Editor: Tim Cooke*
*Design Manager: Sarah Williams*
*Children's Publisher: Anne O'Daly*
*Editorial Director: Lindsey Lowe*

### About the Author

LEON GRAY has worked in publishing since graduating from University College London in 1995. He has contributed to a number of award-winning history titles, including *Depression U.S.A.*, *U.S.A. 1920s*, and *U.S.A. 1950s*, and has written on subjects from natural history to the philosophy of science. Leon lives in Scotland with his partner and three beautiful children.

### About the Consultants

EDMUND HERZIG is professor of Persian studies at the University of Oxford. His research focuses on Iranian history in the early modern and contemporary (post-Islamic Revolution) periods, with particular interests in international history and foreign relations. He is currently working on a book on Iran's foreign policy during the presidency of Mohammad Khatami (1997-2005) and co-editing the *Cambridge History of Inner Asia: the Modern Age* as well as a volume entitled *Iran and the World in the Safavid Age*. He has visited Iran many times in the course of the last 20 years.

DORREH MIRHEYDAR is a professor of political geography at the University of Tehran, Iran. She is known as the founder of the systematic political geography course on the university curriculum in Iran. For more than 40 years, she has been teaching and researching political geography. Her specialty is political geography of the sea, focusing on the Persian Gulf. She also played an important role in founding the Iranian Association of Geopolitics in 2002.

# Time Line of
# Iranian History

## B.C.

**ca 3200** The Proto-Elamite culture emerges, based in the city of Susa.

**ca 2700** The Elamites take control of Susa.

**ca 1900–1500** The Sukkalmah dynasty develops agriculture through irrigation.

**559–486** The Achaemenian dynasty rules Persia; under Darius the Great, the empire stretches from Greece to India. The Persian Royal Road is built from Anatolia to Susa to improve trade and communication.

**330** Alexander the Great conquers Persia. After his death, control passes to the Greek Seleucid dynasty.

**ca 247** The Parthians take control of Persia.

## A.D.

**224** Ardashir becomes shah, beginning 400 years of Sassanid rule. Zoroastrianism becomes the dominant religion.

**642** Arab armies defeat the Sassanids and begin Islamic rule. The Arabs take full control of Persia in 651, on the death of the last Sassanid ruler.

## 1000

**1010** The poet Ferdowsi composes *Shahnameh* ("The Book of Kings"), the Iranian national epic.

**1040–1157** The Seljuks, a Turkic dynasty from Central Asia, take control of Persia, Iraq, and Anatolia. They become the protectors of the Abbasid caliphate and Sunni Islam.

## 1200

**1218** Persia is devastated by Mongol raids; the Mongols introduce cultural influences from East and Central Asia.

## 1300

**1380** Timur, also known as Tamerlane, takes control of Persia; his descendants rule until 1501.

## 1500

**1501** Shah Ismail reunites Iran as the first ruler of the Safavid dynasty. Shia Islam is declared the state religion. Within ten years, all of Iran is united under Safavid rule.

**1514** The Ottoman army occupies Tabriz, the Safavid capital, and makes frequent raids into Azerbaijan, forcing the Safavids to move their capital to the less vulnerable eastern city of Qazvin.

## 1600

**1639** The treaty of Qasr-e Shirin, also known as the Treaty of Zuhab, ends almost 150 years of war between the Safavid dynasty and the Ottoman Empire.

## 1700

**1722** Esfahan falls to Afghan invaders; the Ottomans take advantage of Safavid weakness to claim territory in western Iran.

**1736** Nader Shah becomes monarch of a reunified Iran.

**1796** Agha Mohammad Khan takes power.